We'll tell you what it's

really like

We'll tell you what it's really like

The Anthology

Abbie Younger
Anna Kibblewhite
Cecilia Gregorio
Elsie Jackson
Jazmin Alfonso Fry
Joanna Outhwaite
Jordan Johnson
Maryam Mohsin
Mia Moreschini
Ottavia Tenderini
Poppy Page
Sanaa Saunders
Serena Arthur
Sofia Falco
Sophia Morgan
Yandeh Jagne
Zoë Hart

UKHR.com Ltd

Introduction

There is abundant literature answering the question we are asking; what is it like to be a woman?

We are severely underqualified to tell you what all young women feel like, which is in our opinion, a stance many people writing and talking on the topic should adopt. However, what we are able to offer is a personal account of our experiences as young women. And hopefully from the works in this anthology you will be able to draw a conclusion on what we, as a very small demographic, reflect on, believe in, and ultimately, understand 'what it's like'.

The cover of this book is entitled "Nameless faces" by Cecilia Gregorio.

All of the girls photographed have experienced an act of sexual harassment and/or assault, all have had their identity's diminished and been objectified.

This book is dedicated to Shamiela Davids

To be a girl

Being a girl is a constant state

Not defined by age or fate

Even as peers transition and transform

Girlhood is a lifetime of rage and pain

Never to leave your hands, always remain

Mourning day and night

Over your leaving youth

Ever since age ten

A daughter, mother, sister, lover first

Identity tangled in these words, it's a curse

Forever a woman in disguise, always knowing

More than ever let on, it's a constant showing

Never met my mother, never met my father

And never met their daughter

The fear comes when the bones are lost

Don't know where these limbs came from, at any cost

Fever-pitched dreams of meeting you and me

Meeting you and me, a constant plea.

Spain, 2021

She's going home:

It's only a short trip. For God's sake, I'm being so dramatic; I'm tired - I just need to find a seat. I'll find one next to a woman. 3.9 billion women in the world, why is there not one with an empty seat next to her? No opportunity.

Oh, lucky, two empty seats, backwards-facing, but that's okay.

He was right - I complain too much. He's not always right; he was wrong when he said the thing about my boobs. There are my eyes, my hair, and the love I had to share with him. Heaven forbid I mention my intellectual capacity. Those are good things about me, too: I'm more than my boobs, I'm more than my skin, I'm more than he cared to know about - certainly more than how he made me feel. He loved me, though? Or parts of me, at least. Stop thinking about it; I'm too tired to think about it.

Oh God, who's this fool? Fuck's sake, why's he sitting next to me? No, it's fine; I'm overthinking; there aren't many other spare seats. It's convenient. For him. I'll text mum.

'On train, I'll be at the station in 15 x'

Why is he sitting so close to me? Surely, he's too close. Maybe not. Look out the window, and focus on something else. That sick feeling does not go away. I know it won't, so what can I do to ignore it? I'll pretend it's because I'm in a backwards-facing seat; travel sickness is the worst. It hasn't gone away since the first time I travelled. Eleven-year-old me is so excited to be on holiday. Eleven's quite young, I think, for that to happen. I hope my sister never gets groped. I hope she doesn't get told that it happens to everyone or that she should just get over it, that it's her fault for being drunk, for looking suggestive. Victim blaming; excuse for dooming assaults. I hope she can go for a swim when she's eleven without worrying. I hope she can walk down a street when she's thirteen without a grim man jacking off to her. I hope when she's fifteen, she can go out without Mum being worried she'll come home a violated girl. Probably not. It's a pitiless execution of a young girl's childhood, a new chapter of their stories titled 'welcome to the real world'. Stop thinking about it.

Right now, he's definitely too close to me; why are his legs spreading so much? Stop; I'm only tired. It's not all men. It's almost all women, but it's not all men. Focus on something else. The chapter I'm living through in my story now would probably be titled 'exercise'. Exercising my right to live free from violence and discrimination; to be educated; to own property; to vote; to earn an equal wage. I exercise so that self-defence can make a difference and so that I can run away faster. The exercise of self-control, only saying what I need to, then they don't see me as emotional.

Fuck, fuck, fuck.

Up and down my calf. Why is his foot going up and down my calf? Breathe. Breathe. Breathe. I need to stand up. Frozen. His hand is pawing my thigh. What the fuck? Stand up. Pretend to be looking for someone. A boyfriend, maybe. What if I ring a mate and pretend she's my boyfriend? He's asking me questions now. Where am I going? Has he scared me? What sort of question is that? Thank the Lord, a security guard. Go.

"Hi, I'm sorry to interrupt, it's just would you mind please helping me, that man I was sat with is making me really uncomfortable and-"

He's indifferent.

"Oh, right, just go sit over there instead? Yes, that's fine, thank you. Sorry again for being a bother!"

Breathe. Ideally, sit at the back of the carriage, past the backwards-facing seat. There's a free seat. Next to a younger guy in a red sweater. Great. What is he looking at? My t-shirt is blank. No V-neck, not white he can't see my bra. I'll wear a jumper tomorrow. Mind my business. Breathe. I'm so tired. I'll text mum.

'Are you at the station yet? The train's just getting in x'

She's five minutes away. Why did the guard not do anything? It's his job. Why am I even angry? All security is the same. I was only trying to go dancing when I was offered club entry in exchange for a kiss. Me and my tight ass can skip the line, just give him a kiss. Probably good I didn't; clubs aren't safe. I can't even go dancing with friends, can I? Someone will put something in my drink. Men looking for something, not someone to screw. Women don't have voices in the first place, might as well slur their input even more with a roofie. Too tired to go dancing anyway. Too tired to be angry.

Red sweater boy's entire Instagram feed is just models. Maybe I should tell him it's all surgery and eating disorders. He'd say I'm jealous that I don't look like that. He'd probably rate me a 6/10. That's what the boys at school said after finding out about, God forbid, the three boys I've slept with. Those boys had each slept with six. It's not like I couldn't be an 8 or a 9; I could use my favourite glow-up technique: image editing.

Stop getting distracted; where did the pervert go, keep eyes on him. What if he follows me off the train? He won't. Just stand up at the last moment; he won't have the chance to follow me. What's red sweater boy doing now? A video game. A gross pornification of women, unconvincing sexualization, and unfair expectations. Also, just a laugh. Maybe he should read the news instead. I read the news a couple of days ago. The headline: 'Teenage girl gang-raped in train, 5 arrested'. Coincidentally, that's the script of most of my nightmares.

Oh, red sweater boy is getting off here as well. I have to stand up. Great. Mind the gap. Damn it, perv man has gotten off too. Oh, Lord. Shit, where's my ticket? Where is it? Right, why has perv guy - his trousers are down? This is a first. Imprisoned by his glare while he's pissing. Stood there, dick out, smiling, glaring, evil. I know there's a bathroom not even ten steps away. He won't look away, will he? I wonder if his aim is to piss on me or the gender I constitute? I feel a bit sick. Found my ticket. There's mum. Got in the car.

I don't feel like talking, sorry, mum.

Yeah, I'm fine; I'm just tired.

Spain, 2021

He's going home:

Trains are so long; I can't wait to get home.

Hello there, big tits. Whoops, she saw me look. 8/10. Nothing compared to this girl on Instagram, miles of legs.

I'm so bored; this game's getting old.

Oh, she's getting off at the same stop as me.

What the hell? This man's just pissing in the middle of the platform. That's crease.

Can't wait for some food. I wonder what mum's made for dinner.

WHY EVERYONE SHOULD BE A FEMINIST

"Are you a feminist?"

Not once have I hesitated in answering this question. Of course, I am a feminist. As a woman, I have experienced many instances of sexism and discrimination because of my gender. I believe it is my right to be considered equal to my male peers. I stand for equality between men and women, advocating for women's rights so that we are granted the same opportunities and freedoms as men. Hence, I am often baffled by both male and female responses to the question, "Are you a feminist?": often ranging from "Well, it depends on what you mean by feminist?" to "I want equality between men and women, but feminism has gone too far"; and from "No, women already have rights" to "Feminism promotes man-hating." Not only does this shed light on the widespread misconception of what feminism is, but it depicts the extent to which feminism has been villainised in the media and feminists have been associated with a form of hard-core propagandist radicalism.

"FEMINISM PROMOTES FEMALE SUPREMACY"

A commonly shared view of feminism is that of a movement aiming to promote 'female supremacy' and 'man-hating.' According to a study by YouGov poll conducted in 2018, fewer than half of men and women polled in seven countries agreed that they were feminists. For example, in Germany, only 27% of the participants answered 'yes' to whether they identified as a feminist. However, it is to be noted that when the participants were asked once more "Are you feminist?" preceded by its definition as *'someone who thinks men and women should have equal rights and status in society and be treated equally in every way,'* the percentage of people who answered 'yes' increased dramatically. Drawing attention to Germany, for example, the percentage of people agreeing to be a feminist increased by 33%, for a total of 60% of responses.

'YouGov Results', YouGov, March 1, 2018, https://d25d2506sfb94s.cloudfront.net/cumulus_uploads/document/0b1c4ebn2j/InternalResults_Feminism_Feb18_Toplines_w.pdf

From these results, I concluded that there is a general misunderstanding of the meaning of the term 'feminism.' The word originates from the French word 'féminisme,' whose roots lay in the Old French word 'feminin,' originating from the Latin word 'femina', meaning 'woman'. Because the word itself encapsulates the term 'woman', there is a tendency for people to assume that feminism advocates for female supremacy and promotes man-hating. Nonetheless, if all anti-feminists took the time to do their research, they would find that there is no allusion to female supremacy or man-hating in the definition of the movement itself.

The Cambridge Dictionary definition of feminism:
'The belief that women should be allowed the same rights, power and opportunities as men and be treated in the same way, or the set of activities intended to achieve this state.'

Another definition of feminism by Marriam-Webster:
'Belief in and advocacy of the political, economic, and social equality of the sexes expressed especially through organised activity on behalf of women's rights and interests.'

The key word in both definitions is 'equality'. Put simply; feminism fights for women to be recognised for their basic human rights. There is no hint in the definition of the word 'feminism' to the notion of female authority over males. However, it does call for the deconstruction of a patriarchal system which has entrapped us women in a set of gender norms for centuries. Calling out the oppression we endure because of a male-dominated society is often perceived by men as a personal attack on them as individuals. This is not feminism's intention. It must be said that whilst feminism aims at shifting individual behaviours, it also recognises that sexist attitudes result from an entire belief system built upon centuries and centuries of internalised misogyny. Therefore, as a feminist, I do not believe that women should have authority over men, nor do I vilify men; I simply condemn an unjust societal structure which has deprived me and all other women of equal power and opportunities as men.

Claire Larkin, "What's The Meaning of 'Feminism'?", Babbel Magazine, March 2, 2020, https://www.babbel.com/en/magazine/meaning-of-feminism

As a feminist, I believe in gender equality. Subsequently, one should be a feminist because one believes in gender equality. Advocating for gender equality and rejecting the term 'feminism' are mutually exclusive events. An individual can't stand for one without standing for the other. If one claims that they believe women and men should be treated equally but don't identify as a feminist, I am curious as to what type of equality they stand for, considering that feminism recognises that gender equality can only be achieved by improving women's political, economic, and social condition.

"FEMINISM HAS GONE TOO FAR"

It is often the case that the media showcases a few examples of extreme behaviours on the part of feminists and exploits the incident to generalise feminism as an ideology which promotes radicalism and violence. The repercussions of this unfair and false representation of the feminist movement are identified in a survey conducted by an anti-extremism organisation, the Hope Not Hate Charitable Trust, in 2020. More than 2,000 participants between the ages of 16 and 24 were assessed in the survey, and 50% of men agreed with the statement that 'feminism has gone too far and makes it harder for men to succeed', while 21% disagreed.

The results of the survey expose the impact of the misrepresentation of feminism in the media, and this once again relates to a general misunderstanding of the term 'feminism.' Anyone who advocates for anything other than equality between men and women is not a feminist; the term 'feminism' should be completely scratched by the press when referring to protests, figures or forms of public unrest calling for female superiority and male oppression because that is not what feminism is. Feminism is the belief that men and women should be equal, not that one should dominate the other. Thus, if one were ti state that they do not

https://hopenothate.org.uk/hnh-charitable-trust/

Sabrina Barr, 'Half of Generation Z men think feminism has gone too far and makes it harder for men to succeed', The Independent, August 4, 2020, https://www.independent.co.uk/life-style/women/feminism-generation-z-men-women-hope-not-hate-charity-report-a9652981.html identify as a 'feminist' because feminism 'has gone too far,' they are exposing their misapprehension of the aim of feminism and consequently unravelling the influence of the media in constructing a baseless link between feminist activism and forms of unrelated fanaticism.

Furthermore, in view of the second part of the statement of the survey, there is a widespread misconception that because 'feminism has gone too far', it has made 'it harder for men to succeed'. From this statement, it is possible to extrapolate the implication that empowered females are stripping men of their privileges, placing them at the bottom of the hierarchy. I do not need to explain how absurd this sounds. To suggest that feminism has provoked a reversal of gender roles and hindered men from pursuing their goals is preposterous. Not only does this completely deviate once more from feminism's true intentions, and thus the term should have no place in the context of female superiority, but it also insinuates that women have attained equality and have exploited their equal condition for their own benefit. To imply such a thing is, of course, completely fallacious.

According to the UN's new report on gender inequality, by the end of 2022, 383 million women will be living in extreme poverty, compared to 368 million men.

In July 2022, women held only 26.4% of parliamentary seats globally , and although women account for 39.4% of total employment in the labour market worldwide, they account for only 21% of projected employment gains, drawing attention to the widening pay gap. If anything, the data proves that feminism has not gone far enough. Arguing that women are reflecting oppressive behaviours on men could only result from an equal starting point, whereby men and women are equal, and then one exerts dominance over the other. However, considering that women are clearly at a disadvantage, the foundation for such an argument is absent. Therefore, if one is adamant that feminism has 'gone too far', they have either not

'Progress on the sustainable development goals: the gender snapshot 2022', UN Women, September 7, 2022, p.6
https://data.unwomen.org/sites/default/files/documents/Publications/
GenderSnapshot_2022.pdf

made the clear distinction between feminism and forms of radicalism, or they are unaware of or unwilling to pay attention to the cosmic inequity between men and women, which feminism aims at repairing.

"WOMEN HAVE RIGHTS"

In the past century, women have gained greater freedoms and rights in the eyes of the state, most prominently in the Western world. From the right to vote to access to contraception, from the right to attend University to the right to control earnings and property, the huge advancements in women's rights have enabled a positive progression of the female condition. In the face of such developments, the role of feminism is often questioned.

Why is it that feminism is needed if women have rights? The simple answer is that feminism is required because women are, surprisingly, still not recognised with the same rights as men on a global scale. Accounting for the UN's report on gender equality, it was assessed that although 'constitutional provisions on gender equality, laws that prohibit discrimination against women, and laws mandating quotas and guaranteeing equal rights to confer citizenship are all key elements in ensuring women have equal rights and protections', 'it may take 286 years to secure overarching legal frameworks".

Only 12 countries in the world offer full legal protection to women (Belgium, Canada, Denmark, France, Greece, Iceland, Ireland, Latvia, Luxembourg, Portugal, Spain, and Sweden). Consequently, denying feminism by presenting the excuse that women have rights is a groundless statement. Feminism is crucial because, unfortunately, women are still not granted the same rights as men. Moreover, more rights for women do not automatically establish equality for them.

As a young woman who grew up in Italy and is now living in the United Kingdom, I have been fortunate enough to live in countries which have granted me equal legal rights as my male counterparts. Nonetheless, I am reminded daily of my inequitable position as a female. How am I equal to

Katharina Buchholz, 'Only Twelve Countries Have Full Equal Rights for Women', Statista, March 8, 2022, https://www.statista.com/chart/17290/countries-with-most-equal-rights-for-women/

my male relatives and friends if I am terrified of walking alone in the streets at night and they are not?

What kind of privilege do I have if I am unable to walk past a group of men, whether they be young, middle-aged, or elderly, without them gaping at me, no matter how little skin is showing? How is it that I am equal to men if any party I go to I have to be hyper-alert of my surroundings, keep an eye on my female friends and not let myself go for fear of something happening to myself or others? Is it really equality if I must be made aware of the many more dangers I may encounter compared to my male counterparts when travelling solo in my gap year? I don't feel equal to men.

Women are not equal to men. Referring once more to the UN's report on gender equality, one in every ten women and girls aged 15-49 was subject to sexual and or physical violence by an intimate partner in the past year. Furthermore, an assessment made in 13 countries revealed that 49% of women in urban areas don't feel safe when walking alone at night. Women live in fear. This is not equality. This is not fair. This is not just. As a woman, I need feminism because it is the only hope that I must be able to one day feel safe. Feminism is essential because women don't deserve to face danger purely because of their nature.

"FEMINISM PROMOTES MAN-HATING"
Previously, I was able to counteract this argument by presenting a concise definition of feminism which clearly does not suggest that its ideology promotes hatred towards men, thus insinuating that any form of extremism associated with the notion of man-hating is not worthy of being classified as feminism. Now I dare to suggest that feminism is, in fact, beneficial to men.

According to the Samaritan's latest publication on the number of suicides

'Progress on the sustainable development goals: the gender snapshot 2022', UN Women, September 7, 2022, p.10
https://data.unwomen.org/sites/default/files/documents/Publications/GenderSnapshot_2022.pdf

in England in 2021, the male suicide rate was 15.8 per 100,000 compared to a female suicide rate of 5.5 per 100,000. There are many contributing factors to this substantial variation among men and women, but arguably toxic masculinity and its implications play a vital role in provoking this outcome.

Men face the societal pressure of 'manning up' and being physically tough and mentally strong. From a young age, they are expected to conceal their emotions, as any sign of vulnerability is a weakness. Consequently, there is a social stigma around men's mental health which prevents them from communicating their feelings and seeking support. Men also face the pressure of providing for their families due to their primary role as 'breadwinners.' A survey carried out by Priory Group asserted that the two biggest causes of men's mental health issues are work (32%) and finances (31%).

Therefore, it is undeniable that men carry the burden of being resilient, authoritative providers due to societal expectations. And I am willing to argue that feminism, by promoting female empowerment, alleviates men's responsibilities as breadwinners. Feminism aims to deconstruct a patriarchal structure which has deprived women of basic rights for centuries, preventing them from fulfilling positions of power or authority. Thus, all the responsibility has fallen on men. By logic, extending these responsibilities to women as feminism aims to do, provokes an automatic reduction in the responsibility that men hold, subsequently relieving them of some of the pressure.

A 2020 WHO report comparing 41 European countries established that men's overall health appeared to be worse in societies with higher levels of gender inequality. The study suggests that the 'breadwinner model' is harmful to men's health due to its link to higher chances of myocardial infarction and chronic back pain. It is also linked to longer working hours,

'Latest Suicide data', Samaritans, https://www.samaritans.org/about-samaritans/research-policy/suicide-facts-and-figures/latest-suicide-data/
'Men's Mental Health : 40% Of Men Won't Talk About Their Mental Health', Priory Group, https://www.priorygroup.com/blog/40-of-men-wont-talk-to-anyone-about-their-mental-health

and thus higher levels of hypertension, increased smoking, lack of sleep and less physical activity, all of which are contributing factors to men's worsening health. In addition, gender job segregation increases men's likelihood of being exposed to risks within the workplace. They have higher rates of work-related injury and are more likely to develop diseases due to exposure to toxic substances and nocturnal work. On the other hand, in more egalitarian societies, men and women tend to share the same prognostic factor. According to the study, in Nordic countries, where the dual-earner model has been adopted, and thus there is a smaller inequality gap in productive working hours between men and women, men's health seems to have improved notably compared to Southern countries.

Consequently, there is sufficient evidence to support the argument that men need feminism just as much as women. Men need feminism because they deserve to be vulnerable, they deserve to freely express how they feel, and they deserve to showcase who they really are. As Nigerian writer and activist Chimamanda Ngozi Adichie puts it: *'We do a great disservice to boys on how we raise them; we stifle the humanity of boys. We define masculinity in a very narrow way, masculinity becomes this hard, small cage, and we put boys inside the cage. We teach boys to be afraid of fear. We teach boys to be afraid of weakness, of vulnerability. We teach them to mask their true selves.'*

Feminism needs men in the same way that men need feminism. For women to step up and take power, male collaboration is crucial; in the same way, female empowerment is essential to relieve men of social pressure.

On a final note, I am aware that feminism is not perfect. I am aware of the complexities and contradictions around the movement. I am conscious of

Chimamanda Ngozi Adichie, 'We should all be feminists', TEDx Talks, April 12,2013, https://www.youtube.com/watch?v=hg3umXU_qWc

its Western appeal and of its exclusion of minority voices. And this is something which needs to change and is gradually changing, as more and more women from a range of ethnic, religious, and social backgrounds and a variety of sexual and gender identities are becoming more inclined to take part in the debate. Feminism does not provide all the solutions; it does not have answers to all the questions. Feminism is a constant work in progress; it is continuously changing, it is dynamic, and it is versatile. It is necessary for a better future, for a better society, and for an improved quality of life. Feminism is imperfect. But it's the best thing we've got.

I have recreated real text messages exchanged on a Saturday evening between a friend and I (we are both teenage girls).

Hey have fun

Can you please send your location?

Stop worrying about mee

I promise I'm fine

sends location

Thx

Hey pls pick up

Your phone is going straight to voice mail

And ur phone was fully charged

Pls just pick up

Hello?

Hey I'm really worried now

We're all at home

Please just text me back

Or call

Hey

I'm alive

Aaaa finally

You scared me

What happened?

We had a fight

He was just being a
dickhead

Oh I'm sorry

Where are u now? Do
you need me to pick you
up?

I'm at the hospital

What

What happened?

I'll come and pick you up

No don't worry

I have to stay overnight

Ok what happened

He was just being rl annoying and kept on trying to get me to drink more

And I tried to stop him from drinking but he kept on going

And called me a spoiled sport

I mean I was probably really annoying because we were with his friends and I wasn't drinking

And I didn't want him to drink because he was driving

Hey it's not your fault

He shouldn't force you to drink

yeah but he just wanted us to have fun

I was ruining it

No. He shouldn't make you do what you don't want to do

yeah maybe

I'm really tired

And the pain relief I'm on is super strong

Oh yeah why are you in the hospital?

I jumped off the motorbike

He was driving too fast and wouldn't slow down

Oh my god

I should have your location on permanently

The girl wasn't severely harmed, but she wasn't ok.

This moment showed me how girls always tend to blame themselves; it's never 'his' fault; it's always something we did wrong. This is a tendency instilled in us by society, as it's always something we do that gets us into trouble.

10 women a week die from domestic abuse in the UK alone.

She Was Asking for it

"Without boobs or a bum, you're not hot enough,
But if you do, don't show them off or else you're a
whore!"

"You don't wear makeup? Wear some!
Take that off; that is too much; you look **fake**!"

"Your skirt is too short; your top is too revealing; you're
showing too much skin. **Cover up**!"
"She's not showing any skin; she's **boring**!"

Man winks at the woman whilst going to meet a friend.

"Look **sexy**, look **hot**,
But not too much; you're an **attention seeker**!"

"Men can't **control** themselves,
Men have **needs**!"

"Don't play around too much with men; you're a **slut**!"

"Drinking and smoking is **unattractive** if you're a woman,
But if you don't, you're no fun!"

Car horn beeps at the woman.

"You look like a **skeleton**; why don't you eat more? Men
like women with more meat on their bodies!"

"You're too thin; get thicker,
You're too thick; you're **fat**!"

"Don't be so fat, but don't be so slim.
Eat more; **stop eating so much**!"

"Why don't you just order a salad?"

Man whistles the woman as she walks past.

"You should **shave**; you have too much hair on your body."

"You're trying too hard!"
"Stop being so confident; you're so narcissistic!"

"Don't come home too late; you never know who is outside."

It's dark; a man follows the woman, but it is too late…

"She was asking for it"

Women earn, on average, 16% less than their male counterparts.

The rules women have to abide by

All girls know the dangers of going out.

We all get taught the basic rules the moment we start to go out: don't leave your friends, cover and watch your drinks, don't go out alone at night etc.

And we all try our best to abide by these rules because we know they'll keep us safe.

And we know it's 'not all men', but there is a reason why men don't get taught these rules. Statistically, girls get targeted a lot more; we are at higher risk, and we should be careful because we should be 'better safe than sorry'. Who would disagree with that?

But why do we have to be taught these rules, and why does our life depend on them? We are teaching the solution to a problem that ideally shouldn't exist. However, by only focusing on the solution to this ruthless issue, we will cause other problems.

Spiking drinks has been common for many years, but injecting drugs into girls with needles wasn't, but now it is. This is caused by not focusing on the problem and only talking about solutions we caused another problem.

When I bring this up, most people look at me as if I had three heads: "don't be so silly; who knows what would happen if you didn't listen to these rules" they all say. For the past 30 years, not having these rules has seemed impossible and frankly stupid; many women have relied on friends to get them out of sticky situations where men wouldn't leave them alone. But it shouldn't be this way and doesn't have to.

When topics such as toxic masculinity or rape culture come up in class, boys laugh, make fun of the PowerPoint or the teacher, and take nothing in.

I sit at the back of the class, exasperated and desperate that these boys take this in because for too long has the phrase 'boys will be boys' been used to excuse rape culture and sexual harassment.

And I am constantly told to be grateful when people tell me, "If only you had to go through what women had to go through when I was young, then you would never complain!"

And sure, I may be grateful to live in the 21st century rather than the 20th; however, I think everyone should nonetheless recognise that life isn't perfect.

But yes, my life is better as a woman than it may have been 50 years ago, but that isn't an excuse for the fact that I still get catcalled in the street by men. I still get told to let boys be boys and deal with it, I still get mocked for caring about my appearance, and I still hear people teasing others, saying, "don't be a girl".

Life may be better, yet it is still far from perfect, and I want to be able to do everything men can do even though I am a woman.

Instead, imagine if we didn't have to be taught these rules, and I could simply go out and do as I please without worrying about being sexually assaulted on the street.

By Zoë Hart

Over 1.2 billion women and girls live in places where safe access to abortion is restricted.

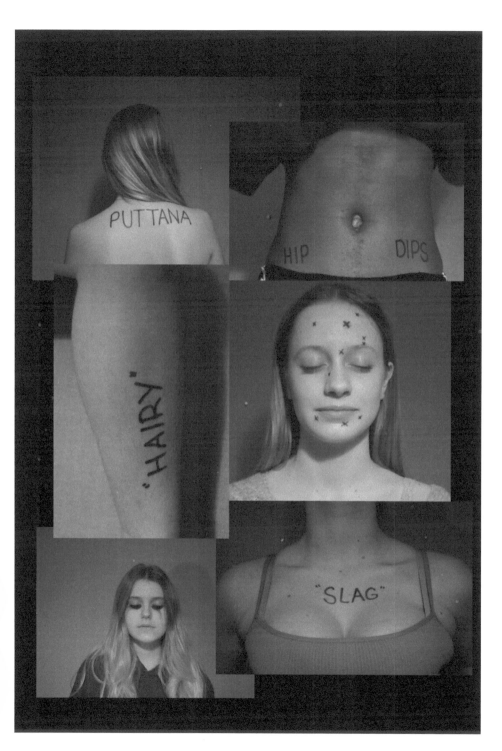

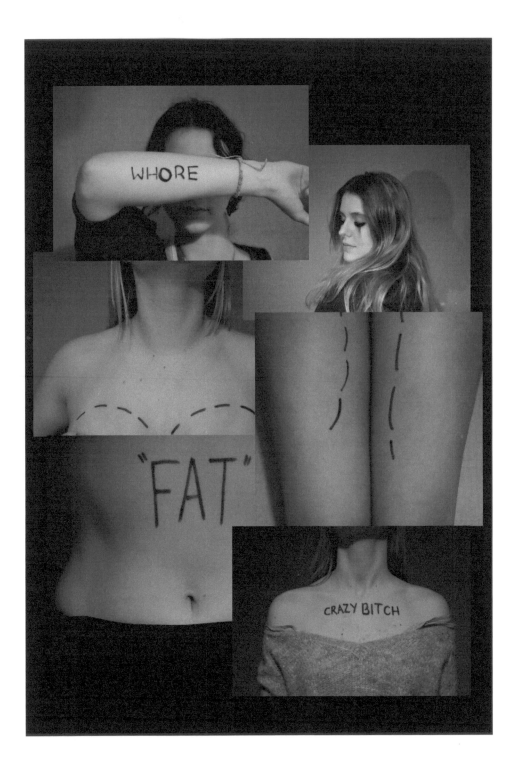

You're here again.

You look miserable.

I see you prodding your imperfections and flaws,

while you rip your self-esteem to shreds looking at a piece of glass.

I feel sorry for you while watching the tears roll down your face.

And even more when you wipe them away and force yourself to believe you are okay.

The Thoughts of My Mirror

I question if my body is the kind they call 'desirable'.

I scroll past the models on my phone and look at the girls my age with just 'good genes'.

And they both eat my hunger away every time I stumble across them.

How f*cking unfair.

The 22-inch waist, flat stomach, and slim legs.

I look down at myself, and we share no similarity.

I diet, I exercise, I binge, I starve, and I tear my self-esteem apart every time I come across a reflection of myself.

And yet, I see no desirability in myself.

So now I drown,

I drown in the overwhelming and constant comparison of every single centimetre of my body to another stranger.

Jealousy

46% of women could not afford to buy both food and period products last year.

Round Cycle

It's a cycle
You're fine and it's over until it's not
And you're yourself
But the worst version of it
The version that's the most comfortable
Because you're no longer on the edge of going back
to it
But after the relief comes the hate
Hatred of how you could do this to yourself
But you don't want to
So eventually you hate yourself again enough to
stop
And then the stage of elation
Because you fixed yourself again
You're fine and it's over

Dear young women of the future,

Another thing that affected most of the young women of the early 21st century was constant stereotyping between the teenagers themselves as well ~~as~~ as the stereotypes pushed onto them by the media. For example, a typical stereotype that is portrayed in the media is that a blond girl is usually shown being stupid and doing stupid things but somehow, they still get everything they want. This gives false expectations about certain things and people come to believe these lies. Other stereotypes that can be related to women are that they are too emotional and that they always seem to be crying. In the media, young girls are also always shown to be reliant on men when they get into trouble and expect them to save them from it. This can lead the young girls that watch these things on TV to be expecting for everything to come to them without doing anything to gain it.

This can also lead to them not being independent which also ~~reads~~ feeds into the stereotype of women always needing other people to do things for them. Another typical stereotype that's portrayed onto young girls like to wear the colour pink. This is not at all true. Pink is seen as a very feminine colour. Different girls like to wear all different types of colours. Pink is also thought to be the favourite colour of most girls. However, this can be debunked as most girls hate the colour pink, as it always seems to be what they are told they should ~~be~~ like. For example, my favourite colour is blue. It's also one of the colours I love to wear the most.

And one of the biggest stereotypes that girls have been put under is that they shouldn't play ~~spo~~ or go to the gym and that these thing should be left to the boys. This is the biggest stereotype that girls have ever been put under as some girls are ~~extrebay~~ extremely good at playing sports. Some of the best sportsmen have been women and they have proved to be better than people would have expected them to be. In 2022, a women's football team called the Lionesses ended up ~~being~~ winning the European Championship for football. However, in 2021 the England male football team lost the European championship which shows that not only men can be good at sports and sometimes women can prove other people wrong.

Overall, young girls should not fall into the trap and believe what these stereotypes say that they should be. Young girls are still able to thrive and experience new things as they still have a long life ahead of them. Don't be afraid of what people might say and how they think that you should not be doing what you're doing. In the early 21st century people started to relax and start accepting the fact that maybe girls and boys were able to do the same things and where not confined to specific activities that were said to be for one gender or the other.

I hope that in your time people have finally comprehended that there is no difference in what a girl and boy can do and that the girls are able to do the same things as the boys. I hope that the young women in your time have realised how strong they are and know how much they can achieve if only they put their mind to it.

Remember to always be yourself and don't let other people judge you and dictate your life.

Kind regards,

Your friend,

We'll tell you what it's like

Today we might not be fighting for the right to vote, but equality and respect are still issues that are unlikely to be resolved soon. It is true that progress has been made and that many women live in societies which seek to elevate women's standards and ensure gender equality. However, the subtle, less noticeable issues need our attention. For instance, globalisation and the rise of social media have created a world in which young girls constantly compare themselves to farfetched ideas of what it means to be a woman. Millions of girls and women feel as if who they are and what they look like is not enough. As if that wasn't enough, we are still less likely to earn more than a man or have access to education. In fact, many women don't even have control over their own bodies.

I am severely underqualified to tell you what all young women feel like, which is, in my opinion, a stance many people writing and talking on the topic should adopt. However, I can offer a personal account of my experience as a young woman. And hopefully, combined with the rest of the works in this anthology, you will be able to conclude what we, as a very small demographic, reflect on, believe in, and ultimately, 'what it's like'.

This is as good as it gets

Although sexism and gender inequality are issues present in every country, I can't help myself thinking that the position of women in the society I live in today is as good as it gets. Places such as North America, Europe, Australia and Japan have the highest gender equality index, but almost everywhere else, women don't even benefit from the bare minimum.

The differences in the status of women in different societies were shockingly revealed to me in my regular visits to relatives in Cuba. Every time I point out one of the many sexist aspects of Cuban society, my father reminds me that 'things are different here' or 'it's a different culture'. But I've always thought it shouldn't have to be, that women shouldn't have to endure cheating husbands with second families just because they don't have the financial independence to do anything about it.

This issue is so common it actually has a name, the two-family problem. It stems from an inability on the part of women to support their families or even themselves without financial input from their partners. It is made even worse by the economic situation in Cuba, where basic necessities are not always guaranteed or are hard to purchase. Consequently, divorcing or separating from your husband in times of hardship becomes financial suicide. Let's say this situation is far from being such an issue in countries like the UK.

There are other differences which, although less noticeable, were just as shocking. For example, my guitar tutor in Cuba essentially told me women couldn't play the guitar in the same position men did, and that they should balance the instrument on the opposite leg to keep their legs closed. It felt horrible to have such a natural thing as sitting be subject to what a depressing old man deemed acceptable, and I cannot help but feel sympathy for the millions of women that go through worse every day.

I was also the only girl in the few karate lessons I joined in Cuba during the summer. On the island, if a sport has been traditionally male-dominated, you are still unlikely to spot many girls participating.

In Brussels, the situation was different, although not by much. I was very sporty as a child; I was just as strong or fast as many of the boys in my year. This gave me a huge amount of confidence in believing that whatever boys could do, I could do it too. My karate teacher, or Sensei, played a massive part in this. "Je peux, je dois, je suis capable", which translates to 'I can, I must, I am able', was a phrase he repeated nearly every lesson. It encouraged me to believe that regardless of my gender or age, I could do anything as long as I pushed myself hard enough. Karate, and sport in general, became a way to prove to myself that I could do anything a guy could.

However, this motivation slowly dwindled. Part of it was because I was the only girl my age at my karate club and the few other women in my class were much older. Despite my passion for the art, karate became a chore. This might not have had such an impact if I'd joined when I wasolder, but the issue was I spent most of my childhood, from age 5 to 15, feeling out of place doing something I loved. The fact that karate was, for the most part, a male sport created an environment which slowly eroded my passion for the sport. And I can't help myself thinking that if it had been a sport young girls were encouraged to do, in the same way, dance or gymnastics was, I would have never stopped. In any case, the result was that I ended up switching to hockey instead, where the only demographic in my team was my own; 15-year-old girls.

A more upbeat version of myself would argue that we should be thankful to live in a society that has at least undergone *some* progress regarding women's standards. For example, being one of the few girls in my karate class was hard in Brussels, but it would have been much worse in Cuba. However, current me is less optimistic and can only view our situation as the lesser of many evils. Maybe I'm ungrateful; maybe my vision is clouded by my own experiences. But that's all this is: my personal experience of what it's like to be a woman.

Jazmin Alfonso Fry

77% of girls over 13 have felt pressured to send a nude picture.

"Ma che, stai sulla Salaria?"

We're all taught what's right and wrong. As a child, I was tricked into the false reality that everyone thinks as you do and that everyone knows being kind and respectful is right.

I then embarked on a new journey, many years later at school, and learnt the rights and wrongs in a legal context. It was inspired by what the teacher told me (a woman who was a prominent figure in the patriarchal Italian judiciary system). She chose to teach because she was passionate about the law and hoped to inspire students to be the same. She would talk on and on about the Italian constitution and how it was written to benefit every person on Italian soil. However, law soon taught me that not everyone has the same perception of what's right and wrong. Instead, there is a fundamental fine line between being a good person and not. Sadly, the teacher who inspired me so much and was a role model quickly became anything but.

One day at school, a friend had a free period, and everyone was chatting, playing, and taking pictures. One girl had come into school wearing a top which showed some of her stomach, which some may consider inappropriate for school; however, we had no dress code against it.

Suddenly the teacher walked into class, took one look at the girl and said disgustedly, "Do you think you're on the Salaria?"

Words uttered by a teacher to a friend, "Ma che, stai sulla Salaria?"

Being told you look like a prostitute is a large pill to swallow. But when it's in front of your class and in school, when you're only showing a little stomach, it is harrowing, humiliating and horrendous.

(For context, the Salaria is a motorway, da6ng back to the Roman era, which crosses Italy from Rome to the east coast. When driving into Rome on the Salaria you will always spot pros6tutes on the side of the road, a well-known fact among Romans.)

It's often been said or suggested by teachers that girls dressed like 'that' to 'distract boys'; being told that from when I was in primary school made me feel disgusting, all eyes are on you, and suddenly you're not sure why you were wearing those clothes. Did I think I looked pretty, or was I trying to attract attention?

Combined with the constant comments from boys saying she'd asked for it and he didn't do anything wrong, she constantly puts the blame on girls.

Again and again, girls get told we are doing things for the wrong reason but are never told what the right way is.

What length should my skirt be then? How should I go out at night? I can't wear this top because it shows my shoulders, but I can't wear this top either because it shows too much cleavage, but if I wear anything else, I'm going to be called a prude.
So what should I do? What is the 'right' solution? Truthfully every single thing girls wear will always be wrong, and there is always something girls should've done that they didn't.

And it takes a while for someone to knock some sense into your head, and even longer for you to do it yourself and realise that society is just not a great role model.

Zoë Hart

This is not a poem

If you sometimes get handsy

If you hear yes when we say no

If your jokes make us uncomfortable

Then you're not a man; you're just a hoe

Jazmin Alfonso Fry

If you know a bit of French or just want to see my Instagram page about sexual harassment on the streets, scan this QR code:

POST SHARED ON 12 MAY 2021
BY PAS_TA_BICHE

12 million girls under 18 are married each year.

Whilst growing up with a privileged background, experiencing private, state, and boarding schools, one element remained constant: gender oppression in the school environment. As a woman in the 21st century, I have first, and second-hand experienced the reality of gender inequality, reflecting the alarming views of the society we live in.

Girls around me were asked at the weekend, "would your mother let you wear that?" when the slightest section of their midriff was showing. The outdated opinions of those in a position of authority in a school environment are shocking and act as a catalyst for body image issues in teenage girls. Body image is listed as one of the top four concerns for young women, but the constant comments on the appearance of girls are still normalised. It is no wonder that 70% of girls are unhappy with their bodies by the time they reach 17 years old.

The media is a constant reminder of what society views as the 'idealistic woman' and the promotion of unrealistic ideals is heightened in school environments. Schools are a microcosm for the world as a whole, in which girls are sexualised for simply having breasts or judged when standing up to oppression. Society is constantly telling girls you are your looks, and schools are not doing enough to eliminate this stereotype.

Going to dinner in the school refectory, I am not allowed to show my shoulders. Yet when boys go against the dress code, the same reaction is not replicated. The contrast in treatment between genders down to issues as small as clothing is frustrating beyond belief.

I remember being new to a school at 17 years of age, and it was the first non-uniform day of the year. I got dressed in the morning, and the first interaction I had, before even entering the school, was, "you should be careful wearing those; they don't like it". The way they spoke to me sounded as though I was wearing 3-inch booty shorts and a top the width of a belt. I was actually wearing jeans. Jeans which had a slight rip in, but granted, you could see a glimpse of my kneecap. I was struck with confusion, and that moment has stuck with me for a long time.

Do they really care that much when girls show the slightest bit of skin? It didn't impact my education in any way, so why would they care? Surely teachers should be more focused on my education rather than looking out for kneecaps.

Despite this, the gender inequality gap has decreased in education: in the 1800s, it was rare for a girl to go to school, let alone study for a degree. Yet women still make up for two-thirds of all adults who cannot read. Why is it that boys had an easier route to education? Just because they had a different set of chromosomes. Although this was a long time ago, this outdated look at the education system has not entirely vanished.

Girls are still less likely than boys to ever enter a classroom, and there are 130 million girls worldwide who are getting no education at all. It, therefore, shouldn't come as a surprise that the global labour force participation rate for women is now less than 47%.

At the age of 11, I was educated on the menstrual cycle in primary school, along with the other girls in my class. But no boys. I was told I wasn't allowed to discuss this outside of the classroom. Aware of it or not, the education system developed a stigma around the natural processes of a woman's body, giving the impression to 10 and 11-year-old girls that it is 'embarrassing' and should be kept quiet. Children are constantly absorbing gender stereotypes, and this endless cycle will not change until something is actually done about it.

As an adult now and looking back at my life as a female growing up in this strange world, I am very aware that my life would look and have looked very different if I was male. But then again, the contrast in the treatment of men and women isn't just apparent in education.

I work hard to gain a good education, knowing that I will be paid 18% less than a man when I get a job simply because of my gender. The issue of gender oppression and inequality is around us in everything we do, from all nurses at school being female to the familiar phrase particularly dominant in primary education, "I need some strong boys to carry this", when physical labour of any kind is required.

The difference between genders is still significant today, tracing back to causes as little as uniform policies and how this fuels society's belief that women are not equal to men.

A question I have been asked an innumerable number of times during my childhood was, "where are you from?"

A question that, no matter how old I got, I became no better at answering. The thoughts that used to run through my head would be wondering how they would want me to answer. Was this where I was born, where I had lived for the longest or where I was living at the time? I felt like I wasn't from anywhere, that no matter how long I lived there, I didn't truly belong. I often felt like an outsider surrounded by people who grew up in the same place.

When talking about this, I used to be told the same cheesy saying over and over again, always something along the lines of "home is where your heart is" or "home is where your family is". As someone with family all over the place, this never truly resonated.

I was told that no matter how lost I felt, I always had people who would ground me. That it didn't matter what the answer to the question was, that I was lucky to have a roof over my head no matter where I was. My sense of belonging has always been a very vague concept, something that has been at the tip of my fingertips, just unable to grasp. I knew I belonged somewhere or with some group of people but never knew exactly who or where. I had just assumed I would find it at some point in my life. But I was jealous of the people who had lived in the same family home since they were born or the people who grew up with their friends and went to all the same schools.

Growing up, moving around so much greatly challenged my resilience; as much as I had to laugh when my parents called the experience character-building (as almost an excuse - maybe they felt bad?). But looking back, from where I currently am, maybe it was. I would not be the same person I am today if I wasn't brought up in an environment like the one I was.

When I was younger, I knew nothing about herd mentality. In my mind, I didn't have a herd to follow. My environment changed so much that I had to adapt and adjust along the way. Sticking out like a sore thumb as the new person at school or moving into an entirely new environment that I wasn't used to gave me no choice but to stand out, and that was normal. As a small child, everyone was different, no one thought about your differences, and no one judged you. But as I got older, it changed; even staying in the same school for seven years, I saw trends change and people along with them.

So now you're probably wondering what any of this has to do with being a woman in the 21st century. I learnt over the years that people thought fitting in and blending in were synonymous. People, in particular women, were sacrificing their beliefs and feelings in the hope that they would 'fit in'. Which I think is a particularly important concept as we have come to a time where everything online is a result of people trying to 'fit in'. People are trying to go with the masses to avoid exclusion or feeling left out. Social media makes us all think that we all must fit in, and blend in; that we all must fit into the same categories, to yield to the same beauty standards we see for hours on end on Instagram or online.

Lots of people have the same view on fitting in, that it is just something people do because they 'change with the times'. However, what people fail to see is how detrimental this can be. Global eating disorder statistics have increased from 3.4% to 7.7%, and eating disorders are the third most common chronic illness among adolescent females. People are almost killing themselves in an attempt to fit in. And somehow, we don't see it as enough of a problem.

It is something I have had to learn the hard way, but something that has benefitted my learning; we aren't all going to fit in somewhere perfectly. We don't have to be a certain shape or size to be able to fit into a box that we tick to say who we are. We aren't defined by what we look like but by how we act; we are defined by our actions and our reactions. The way in which we stand up for what we believe in and how we fight for our place in the world.

It truly does not matter where you are from or how you define it. It is about where you feel you belong; those shared experiences mean so much more than you think. Positive or negative, those experiences are what define us. Not where we were born, where we live, or where we have spent most of our life, but those people who are around us who provide a community. Fitting in is not the most important thing; it's about finding where you feel most comfortable and who you can surround yourself with that will make you feel seen and heard.

Name calling is abuse

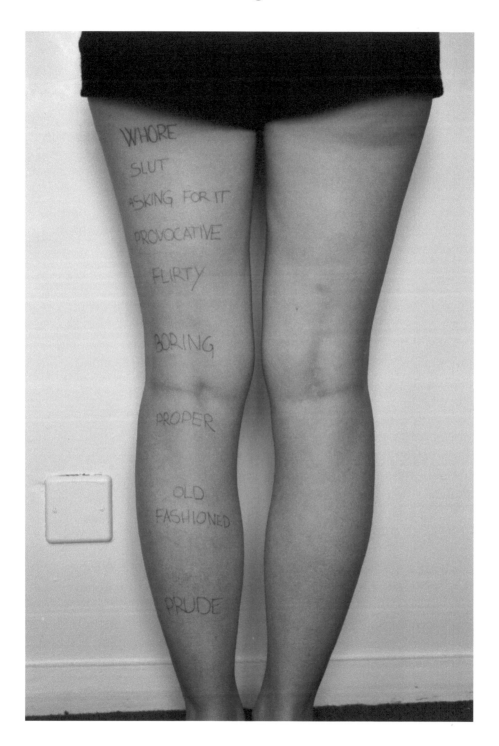

Whore, slut, asking for it, provocative, flirty, boring, proper, old fashioned, prude.

These are merely a few judgements/slurs of a large-scale vocabulary that many people are subject to repeatedly over the course of their lives. In most cases, the receiver is female, and the abuser is male.

I want to add, before revealing a story many females are familiar with, that my choice of words has been selected carefully. If one searches for the definition 'abuser' in the dictionary, they will find this: 'A person who treats another person or animal with cruelty or violence, especially regularly or repeatedly.' One treats another person with cruelty by utilising tools at their disposal. Unsurprisingly, the tool most often used is language or one's voice.

Like all tools, language and word choice have a purpose and an effect. I know that utilising selected words to hurt an individual or an entire community is not always the intended purpose. Yet, verbal abuse is one of the most common forms of abuse. It can include: blaming, condescension, criticising, gaslighting, humiliating, judging, manipulating, name-calling, ridiculing, threatening or withholding.

Although this piece doesn't aim to show the physical and psychological effects of an offensive, undermining or condescending act, not much is needed to relate, IF you are a female.

If you are a male, I respectfully request that you continue reading.

The words in the first paragraph represent some of the many names females, from young girls to adult women, get called when wearing skirts, dresses, or indeed any type of clothing. Each hem height provokes the above names I have heard girls being called, or have been called myself, or have been told of, regarding the length of our clothing and how much skin is being shown.

From a young age, most females have had to deal with the typical example of not having to wear a shirt with sleeves to school. Anything less is seen as "distracting to the boys in the class" as "it draws attention to yourself". The same goes for the bottom half of our bodies. Most females who wear dresses, skirts or trousers wear them to be comfortable, just like when men dress. Yet, unlike men, when in public, they are persistently commented on.

Reading each derogatory word as you go down the leg, notice how they change. The cruelty and even viciousness of the slurs decrease as hem lengths descend, yet all of the names are important.

If a female wears clothes that are too short, she is called a 'whore' or 'slut'. Many stories of sexual abuse are dismissed with the phrase, "but they were asking for it". The response is NO. No one asks for physical or psychological abuse when deciding what clothes to wear.

If you wear your clothes one way, it may be seen as provocative or flirty ('asking for it').

It's a losing game trying to comply with the judgement of others. Because even once you've chosen the believed to be 'good' hemline and consider yourself safe from ridicule, jokes, or criticism, a new barb is thrown at you. From whore to just flirty, from proper to prude, yet again you're devalued and belittled for your choice.

If your skirt is long, you are seen as 'Boring'. If your skirt passes your knees (a standard dress code requirement in most schools), you are seen as 'proper', suggesting you are old fashioned, yet those that conform to the dress code are seen as "teachers' pets" and "suck ups". Lastly, we have 'prude': 'a person who is or claims to be easily shocked by matters relating to sex or nudity'.

There is no freedom in what females wear. Nothing seems ever to be right. The constant pressure to conform to whatever society's idea of fashion is at the time continuously forced onto teens. The way they look, act, and wear are continuously criticised and ridiculed.

What is the true effect this has on half of the human race? Self-doubt, low self-confidence, loss of spontaneity or enthusiasm or creativity. Analysing their choices to see where THEY made a mistake. Chronic stress, body dysmorphia and depression. The list goes on… f there is still any doubt in your mind about the effects name-calling, even 'in fun' and said without rancour or malice, can have on people, I did a survey asking fellow students to explain, in a short phrase or word, how verbal abuse affected them. These are the shocking, verbatim replies:

"Objectified."
"Dehumanized (like a piece of meat)."
"F***ing fed up."
"Insecure."
"Embarrassed of how I was dressed."
"Uncomfortable."
"Anxious about showing skin."
"Disgusted with how I looked and felt."
"Inhumane."
"Ashamed."
"Confronted with my body image."
"Hopelessness."
"Guilt."
"Utterly disgusted."
"Disappointed in our failed society."

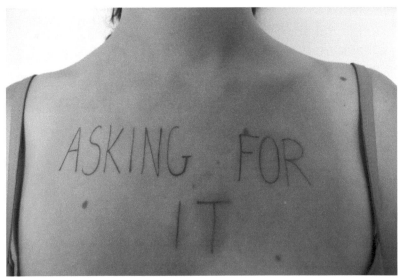

One of the most exposed and looked at body parts, and the message men seem to interpret.

Just like skirts/dress lengths, high heels are also being criticised and judged.

- Slut
- Flirty
- Boring
- Prude

Without fail, we can see how sexualised and harmful women and even young girls are when subjected to verbal abuse. Self-confidence and self-esteem decrease, whilst the abusers' ego increases. After all, they are just doing it for 'fun and games'. The quote, 'it was only a joke!' often doesn't feel like that to females as the female-male power struggle between perpetrator and victim rears its ugly head.

The first time a female experiences verbal abuse will always remain with her and will often even affect how she views her body and her self for the rest of her life. We must do better.

Things I Thought When I Didn't Know What Feminism Meant

Feminism
(ˈfɛmɪnɪz(ə)m) [f. L. fēmin-a + -ism.]
2. [After F. féminisme.] Advocacy of the rights of women (based on the theory of equality of the sexes). (Cf. womanism.)

I Believed All Feminists Hate Men.

This was, perhaps, one of my less reasonable thoughts. A key misconception here is that feminists are trying to create some type of matriarchal utopia or, even better, a place where gender roles are reversed. There are times in my life when I think about how desirable the latter sounds, but this isn't what feminism is trying to achieve. The world in blue encapsulates the true meaning of feminism, something I must've missed at thirteen.

I Thought That Feminists Couldn't Be Feminine.

At thirteen, feminism seemed to be the antithesis of all things that were important to me: dresses, makeup and the colour pink (the list hasn't changed much at seventeen). Still, I know now it is perfectly possible to enjoy these things whilst being a feminist. Feminism means having the option not to wear dresses or makeup or like the colour pink. Being an advocate for feminism simply means not having these 'feminine' ideals forced on you but being able to choose.

I Believed Feminism Was White.

It's difficult to understand my thought process behind this point without me giving you an introduction. I'm black and have spent a portion of my life in Ghana. So, I guess it might be easier for you to see how I fell prey to this notion. Feminism isn't, or shouldn't be exclusively, white. Though the movement still has some changes to make, an intersectional approach which encourages people to understand their privilege, which helps tackle the issue for *all women*.

I Understood Feminism to Be a Third World Issue.

Some people (myself once included) view feminism as unnecessary in today's society. However, it is important to recognise not all societies reflect our own. Understanding that feminism's progress in some places doesn't influence the progress of others. However, first-world countries still have progress to make, too. America has never had a female president, there is still a pay gap between women and men in the UK, and women were only given the right to drive in Saudi Arabia in 2018. But I guess feminism shouldn't be that important to us.

One woman or girl is killed by someone in her own family every 11 minutes.

A diary of an actual black girl

I am writing this on October 5th 2022, and I was just called 'blackie'. Yes, you heard me right; I said blackie.

For context, I am a dark-skinned 5'6" girl who usually has long waist-length braids in, and I am proudly Nigerian. I go to a predominantly Caucasian school, and out of all the black people in my year, only seven have lived in their national country (that includes me).

Walking into school on the first day was terrifying yet exciting. I expected to meet many Nigerians that have lived in Nigeria because, after year 11, most students move to England to take their 6th Form (Nigerian 6th Form Colleges are not seen as serious in the eyes of the universities), but unfortunately, that wasn't the case.

I wasn't very phased because I thought that it might allow me to learn about different cultures and get to understand different perspectives of the world. I am a relatively shy person unless I am spoken to. I have the 'if you don't talk to me, I won't talk to you' attitude; I know it's horrible, but that's what I'm used to.

You can imagine how quickly I made friends. I gradually started to integrate and make a couple of friends and a lot of acquaintances towards the end of year 12, but in year 13, I started to socialise much more (even with the guys). That's another thing about my school culture is that boys and girls don't integrate much. To me it is quite strange because in my previous school the boys and girls were extremely close (almost like family) and if you walked with the opposite sex around the school there would be no speculation that the two people involved are in an intimate relationship, but it is quite the opposite in this school.

Because of my close relationship with the guys in my previous school, that made me extremely susceptible to 'banter', and as you can imagine, most of it was about my skin colour, sprinkled with a couple about my gigantic forehead. The most common ones were when the room was dark, they said that they couldn't see me or that I should smile so they could see me or that I looked like a black hole etc., all the boring ones.

Some more creative ones were that I looked like Gorilla Grodd or that my forehead looked like a chocolate-glazed doughnut hole from Dunkin Donuts, those are some of the more creative ones, I mean, if you are going to take a shot at me least make it unique!

Anyway, that's beside the point. At the beginning of this banter, it really used to get to me. It almost destroyed my self-esteem. But eventually, I became numb to it. I know that is not the healthy thing to do, but it gave me the ability to laugh with them instead of them laughing at me. Whenever they made those sly remarks, I would respond by laughing and telling them to shut up. Once I became numb to these remarks, I formed friendships that lasted over 5-6 years.

Fast track to today when I was called 'blackie'. I was sitting down with a couple of acquaintances in business management class (all of them male, four from Africa, two from Australasia, and another from England). We were cracking a joke about the way the teacher talks, as usual, when one of them (from Africa) stopped talking and glared at me. He stared at me like I had a massive cockroach stuck on my face, and he was trying to find the most humane way to slap me in order to get it off.

Then he mutters to me, "You're so black".

Surprisingly, I was not shocked. I simply replied the way I would respond if I was in Nigeria and said shut up and laughed it off. I was then asked if they could call me blackie, and I responded by saying, "you are literally darker than me". I am clearly darker than him, and I have type 4C hair that shrinks so much that it looks like it can't touch my shoulders, when in reality it reaches my mid back, while he is a good three skin tones lighter than me with type 3B spiral curls.

I am obviously joking, and I find the whole encounter quite humorous because it reminded me of home, where this behaviour was normal. But I was only told that this behaviour was not normal at dinner. Because I am in a boarding school, I spend every meal time with fellow boarders, and we were eating in silence when one of my friends broke the ice and said, "Jordan, don't you find the boys behaviour strange?"

I looked at her quite baffled and asked her what behaviour she was referring to, and she blatantly said, "Them calling you black".

Unconsciously, I immediately defended them, saying that it was not supposed to be offensive and was supposed to be banter, and the table looked at me in awe.

Two of them mumbled to me, "That's not normal, especially the fact that none of them are as dark as you."

I just shrugged it off and told them it was banter. When I got back to my room, that conversation kept lingering in my mind. Why am I putting up with something so discriminatory? Why do you feel the need to comment on my skin tone and say it in such a derogatory tone? Why is this comment always directed at females? As I said previously, I lived in Nigeria, and the majority of people that I was surrounded by were black, and I realised that they never said this to men. In fact, comments about physical appearance (especially the amount of melanin you have in your skin) were all directed towards women.

This goes beyond childish banter; this is extremely apparent in the media. People say that they don't like dark-skinned women and follow it up with 'it's just my preference', to all the 'skin brightening' lotions that are supposed to 'bring out your true complexion' with a picture of a fair-skinned girl in the background applying this lotion; to all the popular people in the media that have or have been accused of skin bleaching because of their sudden complexion change to there being a significant lack in dark-skinned girls in shows.

Growing up with all of these negative connotations attached to darker skin broke my self-esteem to the point where at a young age, I would run up to my mom and point to the area right below my palm and claim that I was light-skinned. But on the other spectrum, it allowed people to view dark-skinned as a negative attribute that is undesirable. And this is a trait of society that is normalised which is blatantly wrong. It is extremely disheartening that it has taken me 17 years to come to that realisation.

More than 200 million girls and women alive today have undergone female genital mutilation.

Being a woman

So, she's useful to you when you're bored

she's useful to you when she isn't there

she's useful to you for her body but nothing more

you say you miss her but use her for your enjoyment

she was drunk and you took that as an invite into her pants

she pulled away you took her in

you saw she was hurting but chose not to see

you saw she was passed out but chose to leave her there

you chose to argue with her, how she overreacted
Maybe she did

You asked for a hug to stop you from shouting.

A hug.

That did not mean holding her waist or her ass so tight she could
not leave.

She asked you to let go

But her words had no affect

you chose and she had no say

You said it was her fault
Of course, it is

Everything you did she provoked you
So of course, it's her fault
But it is what it is because boys will be boys.

130 million girls do not have access to any education.

Growing Pains

Everyone talks about getting older,
The growing pain that is life.
And you don't realise it until you do,
And then you'll wish you didn't.
The truth is that it isn't the milestones that change
you,
It's the in-between of what can happen on a normal
day.
It's not that I passed my driving test,
It's that I could make sure my grandma wasn't
driving.
It's not that I could legally drink,
It's that I didn't want to go out anymore.
It's not that I had the freedom to see anyone,
It's that you only want to see someone who's not
here anymore.
It's not that I turned eighteen,
It's that I only had eighteen years knowing him.

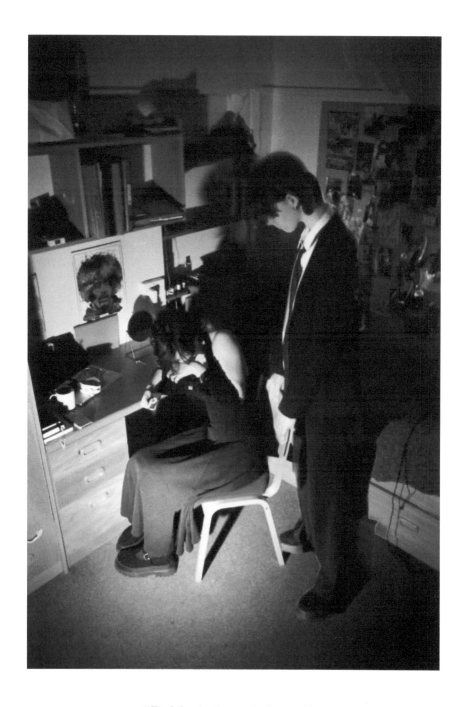

"Behind closed doors"
Photograph by Cecilia Gregorio

Reflecting on gender stereotypes and the effects it has on both men and women. The Pain cannot be seen until behind closed doors.

"Did we ask for it?
Photograph by Cecilia Gregorio

Young women who have faced sexual harassment and sexual assault have been viewed as objects instead of humans.

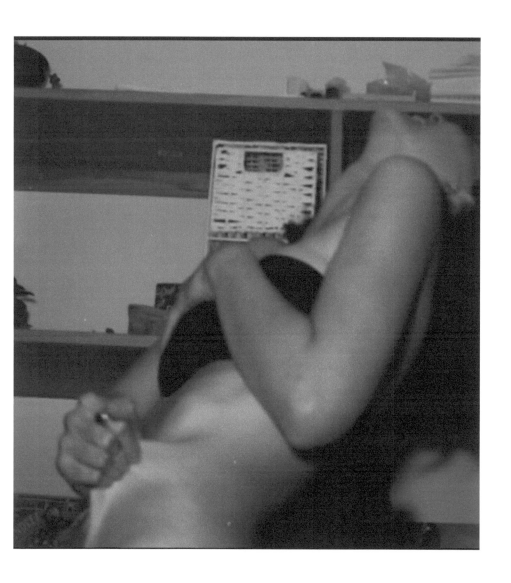

"Under this skin"
Series of photos taken by Cecilia Gregorio

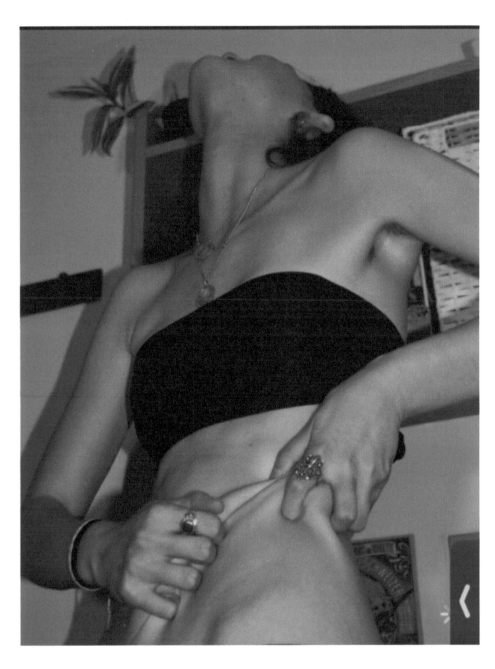

Reflecting on the body dysmorphia of women as a result of society's damaging body standards that women are held to.

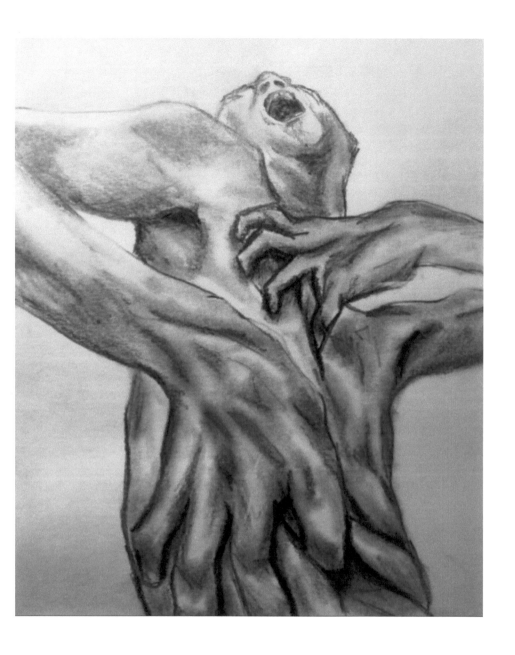

Drawing by Cecilia Gregorio
Pencil on paper

"Under this skin."
Painting By Cecilia Gregorio, oil on canvas.

104 countries have labour laws that mean 2.7 billion women do not have the same opportunities as men.

Integrity

Mediocrity, a state we all fear
But it's not so bad, it's not so severe
I am guilty of wanting more
To feel immortal, to soar

But take me to my motherland
Where my mother's mother lies
Down in the sand
Where my roots are deep, where my heritage lies

Every generation before mine
Fell in love with someone who looks like me
But I'm ashamed to see
The extent I go to, to hide our features

But let me learn to love our face
Let me learn to embrace
My mother's face, my mother's mother's face
Let me learn to face our heritage with grace
Let me face my ancestors
Let me learn to love our face

Model

As a little girl, I often played with Barbies. My sisters and I dressed them up and came up with different life stories for them. Each time I imagined they were living one of my dream lives: my Barbies would swim with dolphins, they became professional surfers, they were astronauts, they were princesses, but often they were models. I made clothes for my barbies, and they always looked beautiful when walking the runway, living all over the world.

I wish I got to live all the lives my Barbies did, but it wasn't like that.

When I was seven, a boy came up and asked me if I was pregnant.

When I was eleven, I was told I could be a model only if I lost a little bit of weight and smiled more; soon after, a friend told me if I stopped eating as much, I could be prettier.

At twelve, I wanted to stop wearing bikinis and only wore full swimsuits because they covered my stomach better. I soon switched back after getting mocked because my legs were more tanned than my stomach.

When I was thirteen, I was told my teeth were too yellow and crooked, so I got braces.
At fourteen, I was approached by a random woman at an airport and told off for not wearing a bra in public.

When I was fifteen, I bought a shaping t-shirt and wore it under my clothes.

Eventually, at sixteen, I finally got diagnosed with PCOS, polycystic ovary syndrome. My medical report read, 'both ovaries appear bulky'. Everything I have ever been is bulky.

My diagnosis finally helped me understand that when I followed a workout schedule and others found it easy to lose weight, but I didn't, it wasn't through any fault in my effort. Eventually, the cause still boiled down to my problem. So I had to find another way. Because if I wasn't skinny, how could I ever be perfect?

The internet claims it promotes body positivity, but if you continue scrolling, you will quickly bump into an article or a video headlined 'tips and tricks to lose weight fast'. I'm told that being curvy isn't something I should be ashamed of, but inevitably all 'curvy' girls have had experiences where they have been made to feel ashamed.

Telling me that I can solve it if I just move more and eat less isn't going to solve my lack of confidence. It would not solve the fact that every time I go into a shop with friends I don't pick out something which may not fit properly, it would be embarrassing if they realised not all clothes fit me.

People may argue that not all models nowadays are stick-thin, but the large majority are. And when a girl who is plus size wears clothes on the runway, all anyone talks about is how inclusive the brand is and how beautiful she is *even though* she's curvy.

The conversation won't be about the clothes, which is what it would be about if the model weighed less, but it is usually either about the brand's inclusiveness or the model's size.

I'm always reminded I should be grateful I live in a world where you can be sensitive about these things because 'back in the day', it was unheard of to discuss these topics. The continuous reminders make me grateful, but they also enhance the point I am trying and get across. We are still talking about all of this, and it's still nowhere near solved, and just because we talk about it more doesn't make it any less of an issue.

Even with the acceptance of "curvy" models in fashion, my childhood dream of wearing the prettiest clothes in the world and travelling around the world wearing them and showing them off is now rotting in a landfill among many other dreams girls couldn't go through with because of how they look.

Women underwent 92% of all cosmetic procedures last year.

Dear young women of the future,

Living in the 21st century for a young women, much like yourself, was probably one of the hardest periods for them to live through. Although they might have enjoyed their years of being a teenager, there where many hard tasks that came with being this age. We all grew up watching TV shows with the beautiful skinny, long blond-haired girl or the beautiful skinny, long brunette-haired girl always being chased after by all the boys and then ending up falling in love with the jock of the football team that was always ripped and the most popular person in school.

However, what this did to the young girls was most probably make them insecure about their body types as well as make them think that there was only one possible way a teenager girl could look like in order to get a man to fall in love with her. This led to many people to either develop a body image disorder, for example body dysmorphia, which lead most girls to think they were fat and so nobody would end up liking them which leads to many other problems such as mental health.

Another thing that this ~~leads~~ led to was girls developing eating disorders. Some of them would completely stop eating as, again, they thought they where fat and so by not eating they would have become the person that everyone wanted them to be. However, this is not reality as they would not eat anything which would only end up with them in hospital, severely sick.

Another disorder that girls could develop is called binge eating disorder and so instead of not eating anything at all, they would keep eating even though they were full. They would keep going until they felt sick that they could literally not stand up as they felt as though they might have spewed everything everywhere. The very sad thing is that these problems would be found in most of the young women as they where put under this pressure from social media and television which led them to believe that that was what was supposed to be normal and that anything else was being fat.

Trust me as being someone who lived through an eating disorder it was a very bad period of my life and the ~~time~~ time that I lost I will never get back. But this is for another time. This was one of the biggest issues that occured within the community of young girls in the early 21st century. As years went

on more and more people started to take action
about this problem and started to create social
media pages that started promoting body positivity
and loving each and every different body type. This,
to some extent, led to more people and mainly girls
to stop caring about what their body looked like
as they started to love their own body. Even though
this did make somewhat of an impact on the issue
but it was still a very big problem.

This problem was getting better as the years went on,
but it would still take a very long time to completely
fix it and would still be a long time ~~until~~ until it
would be completely resolved.

However, something that should be known is that many
people became accepting and worked to try and make
sure all the young girls in the world would feel
happy in their own skin.

Kind regards,

   Your friend,

71% of women have said they have been followed by a harasser in public.

How my culture makes me beautiful

As a third-generation, South-Asian immigrant woman, I can confidently say that my ethnocultural background and heritage have primarily influenced the woman I am today and continue to grow to become.

I can't, however, relate my cultural experiences growing up to that of my grandmother, who emigrated to the UK at nineteen, knowing nothing about the nation she was about to restart her life in. Or my mum, eldest of four, growing up in a largely white, North London neighbourhood in the 80s and striving to pave a path of her own.

Both women have always been, and continue to stay, enormous influences and role models in my life, whom I strive to emulate. Their passion, determination and independence astound me daily. I am aware, however, that the titans I see today, and am in awe of, weren't formed overnight. It has demanded tireless work, struggle and insistence to become the inspirations they are - and that is a story I feel is worth sharing. It is a real and candid one, not shying away from the obstacles that life throws, especially to women of minority descent. It is a legacy not only for me to learn from but countless girls and young ladies who perhaps have felt like outsiders, torn between their places of origin and the places they call home. It is a narrative that illuminates one that is often brushed past. One that empowers women of colour in a society dominated by white and gender privilege.

My grandmother, a born and raised Bangladeshi woman, grew up the eldest daughter of thirteen siblings. In a society and time very different to my own, it was her responsibility to help raise and run the household. So from a young age, she had been exposed to a level of maturity I can hardly fathom. Her childhood was short-lived, as she mothered her siblings, laid food on the table, and soon was arranged to marry my grandfather.

At the age of sixteen, set to marry a stranger essentially, but known to be a good and honest man, her life changed almost overnight. He was ten years older, a Naval officer for the Pakistani military during a politically sensitive time, and soon to leave for the UK.

After being married, my *Dada* (grandfather) emigrated to the UK three years earlier than my *Dadi* (grandmother) to build a foundation there, buy a home and find a good job. He wanted a stable life for her to arrive to, and so for the first three years of their marriage, they were separated, with perhaps an annual visit my *Dada* would make back to Bangladesh to visit.

It was an emotionally draining period of my *Dadi's* life till suddenly, three years on, at the age of nineteen, she was swept off her feet, flown across the globe, and struck by the actuality of a new beginning. A beginning thousands of miles away from home, a beginning without family and a beginning where she was now considered an 'outsider'.

My *Dadi* struggled initially to settle and battled with the distance and isolation from her parents and siblings. I was utterly moved when she told me of the letters she would write her dad, all the while staining the paper with her continuous tears as she pursued to write.

It made me understand the years of pain she must have endured before reaching the point of joy she is at now, where she is able to call London her home.

Throughout this difficult time, however, defying the stereotypes of hypermasculinity in the 70s, my *Dada* encouraged and empowered my *Dadi* to form an independent life of her own in the UK. He wanted her to have hobbies and a routine away from the house, so he urged her to get a job sewing in the local factory, take driving lessons and immerse herself in the local community.

Despite the initial isolation and difficulty of language barriers, gradually, they both began to integrate within society, find their people, make close friendships that still stand today, and begin a family. Despite the language barrier, they both got by, putting their three kids through private school on bursaries, running a restaurant and juggling the many hurdles of day-to-day life. Phases of financial struggle and encounters of racism and discrimination weren't enough to deter the two from striving for their goals. When I hear of the struggles my grandparents endured, and their ability to persevere, I am filled with immense admiration and pride. The woman with whom I have largely been raised is a fighter since I have grown up living with my *Dadi*, and my *Dada* passed away before I was born.

 She is an encouragement to me, and hopefully, others, that despite trials and the lowest moments in life, it always gets better. She has experienced years at a time without seeing her family, the initial intimidation of a large age gap in marriage, combatted racism, raised three children, and continues to astound me today.

Having lived through it all, she has witnessed the gradual change, till now she lives in a part of London where she is surrounded by people who share similar stories. Living in one of the world's most

A photo of my Dadi and Dada with my dad when he was a baby.

diverse cities today, she is a part of an enormous South-Asian community. Many of her siblings have now also immigrated here, and so a place that once felt like a foreign land has now become home. She showcased how being an 'outsider' doesn't mean you will always stay one. It merely means that you will have to fight that bit harder to belong.

My mum, on the other hand, didn't experience nearly the same upbringing. She, like me, was born and raised in the UK, went to her local grammar school, got into a top university, and has slowly worked towards her childhood dream of becoming a doctor. That, of course, is an oversimplification of a life filled with immense hard work and resilience.

Despite growing up in a predominantly white neighbourhood, when I asked her how she felt about the people she was surrounded by, she told me how it was hardly noticeable. Surrounded by many cousins and going to an ethnically diverse grammar school, which was, in fact, predominantly Asian, she wasn't instilled with the same degree of alienation that my grandmother and I have felt at times.

An experience of her own, which is similar to my *Dadi's* early childhood in many respects, is of how she grew up for a portion of years, in an extremely busy and overwhelming home. In an apartment of only a couple bedrooms, she lived with her three siblings, parents, grandparents, uncle and aunt, and so when trying to find a space of her own or place to study, the bathtub often became her sanctuary. Though it seemed obscene to me when I first heard this, she told me of how to her, it was the norm. Despite being busy, she grew up in an environment of immense love and exposure to her culture, which nurtured and empowered her journey to become the doctor she always hoped to be.

She now implements her work ethic in everything she does, as she juggles raising four kids, running a private clinic and being a public GP while upholding our family home where my *Dadi* also lives and my cousin did until a year ago.

She has instilled the same bustle and loving nature in our home that she was raised by, which is why I am so eager to share my family's story in the first place. The culture and family spirit she has surrounded me by throughout my childhood is a gift that I, too, hope to maintain as I go on.

My mum at her graduation, aged 24 or so.

Interestingly enough, where my mum was able to miss much of the othering that my grandmother endured in her early days in the UK, I, a third-generation immigrant, who would be expected to have fully come to terms with my ethnic and cultural identity, having known nothing but the UK as my home, experienced a lot of racism as a child.

I didn't always live in London, and in fact, for perhaps five years or so, for my dad's work, lived in Harlow when younger. Only a forty-minute drive or so out of London, one of the most culturally diverse and welcoming cities in the world, I was faced with the prejudices and discrimination of a largely white community.

In the early and influential years of my life, I was made to feel like such an outsider and ugly for parts of myself I couldn't change, and a large extent of the comments I faced then still impact me today. I was excluded and compared to crude things for the tone of my skin, while my brother, only seven years old, was called by his school peers *'a black Jamaican boy'*.

After feeling alone, being called a 'coconut' countless times, and even being chased by older students, I began to become friends with the teachers and staff in school, as they were the only ones I would feel less judged by. Still today, I feel the subtle impacts of these experiences, as I feel more comfortable surrounded by adults and often feel social anxiety around people my age. There was no media or pop culture at the time, and still limited today, portraying the beauty of my culture and brown skin. Due to this lack of representation, it was and is so hard to feel beautiful, unlike how white skin and ideals are glorified in mainstream media.

The effects of these early childhood experiences have carried through into my sense of self today, causing me anxiety and internal battles that I am still trying to work through. They are not the only experiences I have endured, as these othering encounters have continued to go on, in secondary school, and now my college in Hertfordshire, but the reason I don't feel them relevant enough to mention, is as they haven't shaped me the way those in Harlow did.

As I have grown up, matured, and learned from women like my

Dadi and mum how to process and combat these confrontations, I'm not made to feel small like I once was. I am slowly becoming prouder and more confident with the culture I was raised in and the melanin in my skin. However, I find it interesting that feelings of being an outsider, which my grandma faced in the 70s, are still so prevalent decades later.

It shows the lack of attention minority groups and women have received over time, which I hope to help change in the future. Our voices deserve to be heard and advocated for just as much as the next: our culture and gender should be enriching facets of our existence, not hindrances.

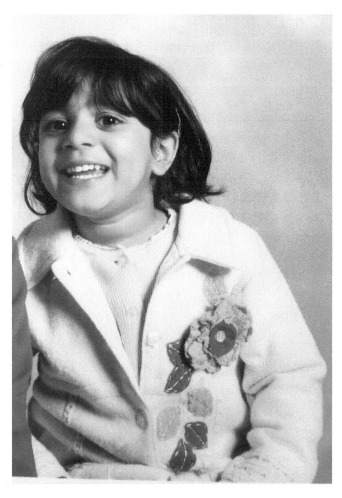

Me, at the age of four or so, when living in Harlow.

By looking through the generational variations and nuances of the experiences of immigrants of varying degrees, I hoped to provide a glimpse of insight into what it can be like as a minority in society.

My retelling is a subtle criticism of the structures of society, but more so a celebration of coloured women despite the difficulties we are made to face.

I hope to be able to read this in years to come, perhaps when I have kids of my own and dream of a reality where societal standards of beauty, ethnic and cultural norms, job opportunities and racial discrimination have all been rewritten.

I hope it doesn't need to take just as much struggle and resilience to feel at home, become a doctor, or feel beautiful, as it has for my family thus far. Though I love and am eager to share my story and those of the women before me, it is telling of how such seemingly natural and mundane life experiences were such endeavours in our lives. That can be put down to the institutionalised inequalities in the UK and, more widely, western society when regarding approaches to women and race. Our womanhood and origins are what makes us beautiful, and I hope for everyone to rejoice in these attributes one day just as much as I do.

Written for enough men

We're trying to tell you what it's like.
And you're supposed to relate.
But you won't.
Because how can you relate.

How can you relate to the ten women every week who die due to
domestic abuse.
How can you relate to the rhetoric of female empowerment when
the reality is keys in hands.
How can you relate the any time of day 'safe home' texts.
How can you relate when my friend gets spiked and spends two
days in hospital.
How can you relate to the fear I have walking around school
because my friend was sexually assaulted in the same corridors.

And this is not for the men who empathise.
It's not even for the ones who may read this.
It's for the ones who would never think of doing so.
As the saying goes: 'it's not all men, no, but it's enough.'

Acknowledgements

We are a group of 17- and 18-year-old girls in an international UK boarding school.

We would like to acknowledge Ted Smith, our editor, for all his time spent advising us on this anthology and Tracy Lewis for her support with this project.

CPSIA information can be obtained
at www.ICGtesting.com
Printed in the USA
LVHW072312010323
740706LV00001B/3